MW01699640

Fleet

A Guide to Simplifying Vehicle Fleet Management for Small Business

by

Sean Lockhart

Fleet: A Guide to Simplifying Your Fleet Vehicle Management for Small Business
Printed by:
90-Minute Books
302 Martinique Drive
Winter Haven, FL 33884
www.90minutebooks.com

Published in the United States of America

Book ID: 160219-00346

ISBN-13: 978-0692726853
ISBN-10: 0692726853

Contents

Acknowledgments

I would like to thank the following people who helped me with the research and editing of this book: Irina Filippova, Thomas Hauck, Jim Davidson, Andy Brooks, Paul Sippis, Magda Taylor and the many professional partners I work with in my industry.

About the Author

As the owner of Lockhart Consulting, a Toronto-based commercial automotive brokerage, Sean Lockhart makes the process of buying new vehicles easy for his fleet clients.

With over twenty-five years of experience in the auto industry, Sean works one-on-one with business owners to lease, purchase, or finance vehicles for their fleets. He understands that many of his clients are just too busy to do all the running around to find the best deal on a new company vehicle. His mission is to save his clients time, money, and eliminate the headaches associated with new fleet acquisitions.

Prior to founding Lockhart Consulting in 2013, Sean had been a fleet manager for BMW, Ford, and Sterling Heavy Trucks, and he has spent most of his career helping business owners improve their fleets.

Sean lives in the Beaches in Toronto.

Introduction

Owning a business can be tough and in order to make a profit, you need to watch your costs and increase your efficiencies. Whether you have one vehicle or hundreds on the road, your fleet can represent one of the largest expenses to your business. In this book, I will share with you what it takes to run a successful fleet and to avoid many of the pitfalls and wrong turns that one can take when purchasing and operating fleets of vehicles.

I started in the automotive industry back in 1990, and most of my career has been in the business-to-business sales. I wrote this book to help business owners simplify the process of purchasing, to reveal the truths and half-truths of the auto business and give guidance based on my experience.

This book will make you look at the true cost of your fleet, stop making mistakes that will cost you money, and improve your bottom line.

By managing your fleet differently and decisively you will have more time for your business and more money on your balance sheet as well.

Ready? Let's get started!

Sean

1. What Toilets Have to Do with New Vehicle Purchasing

Do you want to know something interesting?

Most people would rather clean a toilet than shop for a new vehicle.

This was the basis of a recent Globe and Mail article on the current vehicle shopping experience. This is a clear indicator that consumer opinion of the car buying process is at an all-time low. Shopping for a new car used to be fun, and now for some reason, it has become a tremendous hassle.

How did it get this bad?

In the past, the dealers had all of the knowledge and complete control over the car buying process. Customers went to the dealerships to become educated about the vehicles, the options, and the packages. A professional salesperson would demonstrate and explain the features and benefits of the new vehicle telling the customer everything they needed to know to make a purchase decision. Dealerships at the time were awesome places with shiny new vehicles in the showroom, and it was entertaining and exciting to go there and shop for a new car.

Because the dealers had all the knowledge, they had the advantage in terms of negotiation. The dealers knew the cost of their vehicles and they also knew the worth of your trade-in and could calculate monthly payments for you.

The difference between then and now

Today, the phone in your pocket is a computer that is capable of gathering all the information on any vehicle you want. You have the ability to look up all the options, weights, measures, specifications, and fuel economy ratings. You can even watch YouTube videos comparing models and reviews of each of the vehicles. Sometimes you know more about the vehicle than the person who is trying to sell it to you.

Why it is getting worse not better

Competition has increased in the marketplace, and the dealer's profit margins on new cars and trucks have been eroding steadily for years. To retain margin, dealerships are resorting to adding extra fees and add-ons (doc fees, admin fees, nitrogen tire inflation, theft protection, etc.) that add little value to the client. Now the only way a dealer can stay in business is to go for volume sales, everything is now on a weekly and monthly sales target. The dealer needs to sell more cars and trucks to reach their sales targets. If they don't hit these targets, the dealership will not receive volume bonuses from the factory which they rely on to be profitable. This market and volume based pressure can be a positive development for savvy fleet owners who properly time their purchases

Depending on the size of your fleet, you may have to purchase several new vehicles per year. Would it not be better to plan ahead and take advantage of this situation instead of being at the mercy of it?

Automotive retailing is now over 100 years old, and of course a lot of things are broken, and no one seems to want to fix it. The vehicle manufacturers, dealers, and the customers have become badly misaligned.

The vehicle manufacturers want to build as many vehicles as possible so they can make a profit. Often they force the dealers to take on more inventory than the dealer can normally sell by promising extra target bonuses.

The dealerships then have to sell these additional cars and trucks at a discount to hit all of their sales targets, and once the customer takes delivery, the dealership hopes the customer will return with their vehicle for regular service and occasional repairs to generate additional revenue to make up for the discounting.

What the customer wants is to purchase a car or truck of their choice and to be treated fairly. The customer is spending their hard earned money and expects to be treated professionally and with respect. Based on my conversations with current buyers this is not happening 100% of the time. There is such a push to hit the monthly numbers that many of the steps that would normally make the shopping experience a pleasurable one are being omitted or forgotten. The customer, it seems, has become more like a number than a client.

2. How to Run a Successful Fleet

The first step toward running a successful fleet is to *get organized.*

You should at the very least start with a piece of paper or a spreadsheet to track your vehicles. List all of the fleet by the year, make, and model, and roughly the dates when they went into service.

Next, collect all the paperwork and start making file folders to hold all of the records related to each vehicle: ownership documents, financial documents, and maintenance records. This is a good start; you would be surprised at the number of businesses that don't have even this basic filing system in place.

Do a fleet review

Now that all of the documents can be found in one place, do a fleet review. On your spreadsheet, enter all of the information about each vehicle, including the VIN number, the in-service date, and the warranty expiry date. If there are any loans or leases, add the start date, the end date, the payment amount, and the balance at the end.

Congratulations! You are now ahead of most small business owners. Every time you add a vehicle to your fleet or remove a vehicle from the fleet, that change must be entered on the spreadsheet. This will allow you to track your costs, know the expiration date of your warranties, and the time to replace your vehicles.

Plan to do this fleet review at least annually.

Sitting down with your team, you should discuss the vehicles that are starting to cost more, or those becoming unreliable that need to be replaced.

Do a market assessment

For your fleet review, visit a few websites that list used cars and trucks. Find the make and model of the vehicles in your fleet and record the average value. This will give you a retail value of a fully reconditioned vehicle, though a benchmark amount of its wholesale value should be about 10% less.

There are two reasons for doing this market assessment.

First, you will know the value of your fleet.

Second, you will know whether or not a large repair will be worthwhile. There is no sense in doing a $4,000 repair on a vehicle worth $5,000. Frankly, you should probably not be operating with vehicles that are worth that little money. While some companies subscribe to the idea of "running them into the ground," I have found this to be a flawed strategy because of the higher repair and labor costs that can wipe out any potential savings.

Follow your costs per year

If you look at your fleet costs on a regular basis, you will start to see trends, especially with multiple vehicles of the same type and age. If the costs start to increase on one vehicle, then chances are that similar vehicles will need repairs. If the repairs are minor and you can keep the vehicle on the road, then make the repairs; if you know the repairs will be major in the future, then it's time to move on.

Remember, *the best time to sell a vehicle is while it's still running well and has some life left in it*. Once it's broken, you have to fix it or take a lot less value for it as a trade-in. If you sell it before something major happens, somebody else can then experience the high cost of used vehicle ownership and you can avoid any unnecessary sunk costs.

Keep track of your warranties

You need to keep on top of the warranty expiration dates on all of your equipment. I can't stress this enough because I've seen the following scenario happen so many times over the years: a truck has a recurring engine or transmission problem that goes on for many months and it never gets brought into the dealership for repair. Then a few weeks after the powertrain warranty expires the vehicle stops working. At this point the manufacturer is no longer obligated in any way to fix it, so now the client is stuck with a bill of thousands of dollars when it would only have taken a few minutes to make sure that there was still a warranty on the vehicle.

Get asset management software

There is plenty of good software available to keep track of your fleet and assets. Prices vary from free (one or two units) to thousands of dollars per year depending on the company and services they offer. Choosing the right type of software will depend greatly on the size of your fleet and how much information you want to keep track of.

The key to any software database is that it needs to be set up and used properly. If it's too complicated or takes too long to enter the information, then your people won't use it. Simple is always best so I would recommend to start off with just the basics and you can build from there. You can only improve what you can measure. If you can lower your vehicle costs that savings goes straight to the bottom line.

How much do you *own* and how much do you *owe*?

Using the spreadsheet with the retail market value of your vehicles, you now know what you *owe* and what you *own.* You need to know exactly what you owe on each vehicle every year to assess the value of your fleet. In addition, you should not overstate the value of depreciating assets on your books. You should have an idea of the cost to replace those assets in the future.

Sometimes business owners complain to me that they owe more on their vehicle than it's worth, but the amount they owe on the vehicle has nothing to do with its value. Typically, this situation is due to improper financing or leasing.

If structured properly with the right depreciation per month, some equity should be left at the end of the term. Nearly all cases of no equity are due to overly long terms. The current trend is to extend the term of loans or leases longer and longer, giving the client low payments and the perception of a great deal. Four years later, when the clients owe more money on their vehicle than its resale worth, they think they were deceived. In reality, they wanted a low payment and didn't care about the true costs.

When you think about it, commercial vehicles should never lose money. The amount of money earned by a commercial truck should greatly exceed the monthly payments and costs. It is better to accelerate the depreciation and have some room if you need to shrink the fleet, than to be stuck making payments on that vehicle you don't need.

Know where you stand and have a plan

One example of a process change was a large construction company that owned hundreds of vehicles. They used cargo vans for their employees and would keep these vehicles on the road until they died. They travelled a lot of kilometers per year and they would patch them up and keep running them as long as possible (till they were dead). Each time a van would break down with a major repair like a new engine or transmission, the company had a process.

The driver would have the vehicle towed to the closest dealership. The dealership would assess the vehicle and report the necessary repairs back to the construction company. This would then take a day for the repair estimate. The driver of the van would now have to ride along with another employee until he got further instructions.

Once the estimate for the repair was sent over (say it was $5,000 for a new engine), there were now several layers of management that would decide whether to fix the vehicle or replace it. This decision could take up to a week.

If management decided the van needed to be replaced, it could take another week for them to get 3 quotes, approve the best offer, locate a van, and get the employee back on the road. This was a big waste of time for the managers and the employee. Without his own van, the employee would still be working, however, he was now riding around with another employee until they got the current van situation figured out.

Every time this happened, it cost the company far more than the value of the repair. Even if they decided to repair the truck, the cost of repair and the cost of lost productivity added up quickly. This could be as much as $9,000 for repairs and total lost revenue.

The only way that they figured it out was because it happened so often. Once it was realized what they were doing, to their credit the policy changed quickly. Now if an older vehicle breaks down, it goes to the shop and gets quick assessment. Any minor repair is fixed right away, if any major repairs are needed, the van gets instantly replaced. With a phone call, a pre-negotiated replacement van is delivered the next day. If the older vehicle is repairable and will provide a few more years of reliable service, they will fix it. If not, it gets scrapped.

This company learned what most businesses never learn - the vehicle is the cheapest part. The productivity of the employees and the labor hours lost are the most expensive part. Trying to stretch out a vehicle too long with the high cost of repair was costing them a fortune. They now make sure to replace their vehicles *before* they fail, not after. It is better to get some trade-in value than to have a $9,000 loss. This change in mindset has saved the company a tremendous amount of money since its implementation.

What are your company vehicles silently telling the world about your business?

Keeping all vehicles can cost business owners more than just money. Another cost that cannot be easily measured is the statement made by the vehicle about your business and your services. When I see a technician come to work dressed in a clean uniform and driving a bright shiny vehicle, I think, "That's a professional organization." Conversely, if I see a poorly dressed technician driving a rusty old truck with faded lettering on the side, I automatically assume poor quality and lack of professionalism. Isn't that right?

The guy in the rusty truck may be the best at what he does while the other guy is completely incompetent, but unfortunately, most of us judge a book by its cover. It may not be necessary to buy a new vehicle every four years, but I do recommend that you clean and detail your vehicles twice per year, or at the very least annually.

There are several reasons for this. First is the optics. A clean vehicle with shiny tires says to the world, "I'm ready for business."

Second, in the process of detailing the vehicle, any bodywork or imperfections can be addressed and that will improve the resale value of the vehicle.

Third, your employees will treat the vehicles better. Most employers think that the employees should clean the vehicles and keep them nice. Realistically, if an employee gets a dirty vehicle and they didn't make the mess in it, he or she won't clean it up. Most office environments have cleaners that come in every night to clean, vacuum and dust. This makes things nice for the employees the next day.

At the very least, when you give an employee a new vehicle or pass down an existing vehicle, make sure that it is clean the first day they will be driving it. Let them know that you will be checking the vehicle from time to time and inspect it for cleanliness and damage (and actually do it!). Take pictures with them at the time you give them the keys as proof of how the vehicle was received and what your expectations are. Place the photos in the file and put the time and date on it. All finger pointing is now removed.

Let's face it, employees do not think like you; they're employees and you are thinking like an owner. If the employee thought like an owner, they would not be working for you - they would have employees of their own.

Having a full detailing of your vehicles, twice a year, shows the employees that you care about their work environment and that you expect the vehicles to be kept clean. After the vehicle has been cleaned, there should be no excuses for mud and coffee stains inside. Any mess that happens in the truck is now their mess and their responsibility.

If you give an employee a truck that was driven by another employee, have it cleaned or detailed prior to them getting the vehicle. Review the vehicle with them once again to check for any damage or anything that needs to be addressed and get them resolved right away. This will go a long way toward showing to your employee that you care. It will also make you a lot of money too, happy employees treat your customers better!

3. The High Cost of Saving Money

When purchasing a vehicle, you can't get too wrapped up in the deal. Losing sight of the amount of *time* spent on a vehicle purchase can be costly. Time is a precious resource, and spending too much time on tasks with small payoffs like trying to save a few hundred dollars and spending eight hours to do it does not make sense.

Many entrepreneurs see themselves as master negotiators and they think that sitting down and working out a deal on a new vehicle is a good use of their time. Vehicles can be a big capital investment, and no one wants to pay too much for a vehicle. The problem is that spending too much time on shopping and negotiation can be a "time vampire"; it can consume so much time that any of cost savings will be lost.

"I will have my employee do the shopping and the research."

This scenario gets played out far too often: the owner sends an employee to do some fact-finding and/or shopping. The employee then goes from dealership to dealership, collecting brochures to get prices and specifications. After spending the better part of a week to do all of the research on company time, the employee meets with the owner of the company to tell him or her the good news.

Expecting praise for a job well done in saving the company money, the employee too often finds out that the boss will then repeat the same task by pricing vehicles and negotiating. Since it's the owner's money being spent, they will show the employee how it's done.

So now the owner repeats the same tasks and attains the same results, but with two additional outcomes. He has crushed the employee's morale and made sure that the employee will never try to help again. In addition, the owner has doubled or tripled the amount of money spent on the purchase of a vehicle in wages, plus the overall loss in productivity for him and his employee.

All of this to save $500 to $700 off the price of a vehicle.

Why would the owner ask a subordinate to do a job that he knows he will take away from the employee? If the owner had only wanted information and would not let anyone negotiate on his behalf, he should have been clear about his expectations from the beginning.

This issue may not have seemed like a big deal to the owner of the company but it certainly would be to their employee. The owner said that he trusted the employee to do the shopping for the company, but when the employee reported back the results, the owner demonstrated that he did not trust him at all. It would have been better if the owner had never asked in the first place.

I feel that this situation relates to a zero-sum, win-lose mentality. The owner thinks, "As the owner of the company, I can't show the employee

I'm weak. I need to get a price lower than the employee got. If I don't show them that I beat the dealer, then I'm a loser."

In actual fact, it does not make him a winner to spend thirty-five hours ($3,000 in real wages) in negotiating the lowest price on a cargo van to save $700. It doesn't make any sense and is a waste of everybody's time, and yet this goes on every day.

Price is important, but it is not the only cost

Some business owners spend all their time worrying about making bad deal, so they spend endless hours of back-and-forth negotiating, going from dealership to dealership.

Some people like to negotiate. That's fine, but just keep in perspective that the purchase price does not represent the total cost of the vehicle. Negotiating a great price does not always equal the lowest cost.

The real expense involved in buying a vehicle is a combination of many things. Cost consists of the negotiated purchase price, monthly payments, and the terms and conditions of the contract. The ongoing expenses include the repairs, maintenance, fuel cost, and productivity.

Another cost is employee satisfaction. Making sure that this is a right vehicle for the employees is very important to your success as an owner. Ignoring the needs of the people who work for you can lead to many unforeseen expenses. If the vehicle doesn't work right, doesn't have enough room for tools, is laid out poorly, or is just not reliable, your employees will sense that efficiency and excellence are not your top priorities.

If the employees hate the new vehicle, you will learn to hate that new vehicle as well, regardless of how good of a deal you got.

The right tool for the job

Buying a new commercial vehicle is like buying a new tool to get the job done. A smart owner would not send his employees to cut down a tree with a dull axe or a rusty chainsaw. You would be better off to send them out with a quality chainsaw, the best that you can afford, that will cut down the tree quickly so the employees could move on to the next job.

Keeping the wrong or outdated tools for the job will erode employee satisfaction. If you currently don't have employee satisfaction, then I guarantee that you won't have customer satisfaction either. Happy employees give great service, and they look at your clients as if they were their own. If your workers are not happy, then you'll be constantly fixing mistakes or making additional concessions. This cuts into the bottom line.

4. Which is Better: Financing or Leasing?

Which is better: financing or leasing?

Good question.

It really depends on your company's cash situation. If you have a surplus of cash and you have no debt, you should probably pay for your vehicles outright.

However, the majority of businesses are not in that situation, and they need to finance their vehicles and equipment. With financing, all vehicle loans in Canada are completely open-ended and you can pay them off at any time with no interest penalty. These loans are what they call simple interest, and are not frontloaded like a mortgage. For example, if you choose a four-year term for a vehicle loan and pay it off in exactly one year, then you only pay one year of interest.

Leasing a vehicle improves your cash flow. Because you are not amortizing the entire amount of the purchase, a lease puts you in a better monthly cash position. Payments on a lease are typically lower because you are only borrowing the difference between the price and the residual value of the vehicle at the end of the lease.

If we take a $50,000 commercial vehicle and finance it over 48 months with a 5% interest rate, the payments will be $1,301 per month. If we lease the same vehicle over 48 months at the same interest rate with a $20,000 residual (40%), the payment would be $875 per month including HST (lease payment $774 plus HST = $875). That is a difference of $426 per month.

You could take his extra $426 per month and use it for other expenses in the business. Having a $20,000 residual value on the lease increased the cash flow and put $426 per month back into the company's budget.

Open-end and closed-end leases

There are two types of leases: one is open-end and the other is closed-end lease. For commercial buyers the majority of leases are open-ended, while most consumer leases (cars, SUVs and light trucks) are closed-ended.

With an open-end lease, you, the lessee, are guaranteeing the lease end value. This means if the residual (lease end value) on the vehicle is $20,000 and the vehicle's market value is worth more than the $20,000 residual amount then you keep the equity. Conversely if the vehicle is worth less than the $20,000 you will have to make up the difference and write a cheque.

Typically, these types of open-ended leases have lower residual values than a closed-end lease and they have no kilometer limit. They work well for companies who want to lease vehicles, increase their cash flow, and keep the assets off the balance sheet. If they are structured right they are considered a rental and not a purchase and therefore not a liability.

A note of caution: you need to make sure that the lease is structured properly and that the residual is not too high that the vehicle will never be worth what the residual value is and also not too low that the CRA does not consider it a lease.

Closed-end leases are more popular with consumer leasing. Sometimes called a "walk-away" lease, this type of lease allows you to return your vehicle at the end of the lease and have no responsibilities other than possible payment of excessive damage or mileage charges. The lease has a mileage restriction, and the lessor - the company that leased you the car - is responsible for the residual value. There are limitations in terms of wear and tear of the vehicle. Under the terms of the lease, you are responsible for the maintenance and repair of the vehicle and you must keep its mileage under the limit. At the end the lease, as long as the vehicle is in good condition and does not have any excess wear (this means it does not have four bald tires and a broken windshield), you can return it, even if the actual value of the vehicle is less than the residual value determined at the start of the lease. The lessor assumes a resale risk, not you.

If you want to lease a pickup truck for light duty these work great. However, if you want a pickup truck for commercial purposes like snowplowing or construction, you need to disclose this to the lessor. If not, you may have low payments for the first 4 years and then get huge bill for excess wear and use.

Regardless of the type of agreement you enter into, whether it be an open-end or a closed-end lease, you should know what is right for you and what mileage and wear the vehicle will experience.

Open-end leases are for commercial use while closed-end leases are for light duty or personal use driving.

Which is better when it comes to writing off a vehicle for taxes - purchase or lease?

How much can I write off on my taxes? Whether you purchase or lease a business vehicle you can write some or all of it off. How much depends on the type of vehicle and the way you pay for it.

I do occasionally hear people say that their business vehicle is a 100% write-off. Sorry to burst any bubbles, but you can only write off the business portion of the vehicle and only save taxes based upon your tax rate. If you have been writing off 100% of your vehicle, get out your chequebook, mail in the taxes you owe, and apologize to the CRA for your error.

Disclaimer regarding the following "Class 10 vehicle" tax discussion:

Please do not take tax advice from me or any person who is not a tax professional. The tax laws could change tomorrow, and what I have written here may no longer be true anymore.

Under the current tax code in Canada, passenger vehicles are referred to as "Class 10 Deduction." A Class 10 Deduction is a vehicle that has more than two seats, such as a car, SUV, passenger van, or pickup truck. The tax deduction limit for these vehicles is a pre-tax purchase price of $30,000 and if you lease it, $800 per month. Please note only the business portion becomes tax-deductible. If you purchased a $30,000 personal use vehicle for your business, up to $30,000 of that vehicle price can be deducted from your company's taxes based upon its use (they even allow the HST and the interest up to around $300 per month). There is a bit of a catch, in the first year you can only deduct half of the 30% of the annual deduction. So in year one you can deduct $5,085 (15% of the $30,000 plus HST), and then in year two you can write off the full 30% on a declining balance, which is $8,645 (30% of the $25,500 plus HST).

The good news is that you can take this deduction for the full year in December (as long as the company is older than 12 months). So if your fiscal year end was December, on December 31 you can write off the $5,085, and then in year two write off the $8,645, so you get a deduction of $13,730 in 366 days of owning the vehicle. Not a bad deal! So it makes sense to plan your purchases based upon your tax season.

If you lease you can write off $800 per month plus HST = $920 per month for a total deduction of $10,848 per year. On a lease, that deduction remains constant throughout the term. Luxury cars do have a limit of $546 plus HST on a lease for vehicles that have a manufacturers list price MSRP over $35,294. Please speak to your tax professional to get proper advice and learn what is right for your company when it comes to writing off your "Class 10" vehicles.

What about commercial trucks or non-passenger vehicles? Under the tax code, a commercial vehicle is considered "Class 10.1" this is a vehicle with 2 or less seats and has no deduction limit because it can only be 100% commercial use.

Here is a 48-month comparison of a $50,000 commercial vehicle for both financing and leasing. (Class 10.1)

48 Month Comparison	Financing	Leasing
Purchase Price	$50,000	$50,000
HST	$6,500	$0
Total	$56,500	$50,000
Payment	$1,301	$774
Monthly Lease HST	$0	$101
Total Payments	$1,301	$875
Residual/Buy Back	$0	$20,000
	Tax Deductions	
Year 1 Tax Deduction	$8,475	$10,498
Year 2 Tax Deduction	$14,408	$10,498
Year 3 Tax Deduction	$10,085	$10,498
Year 4 Tax Deduction	$7,060	$10,498
Total Deductions	$40,027	$41,993
100% Business Use	$40,027	$41,993
25% Tax Bracket	$10,007	$10,498
Tax Savings per mo.	$208	$219
Monthly Cost Per Mo.	$1,093	$656
Total Payment	$62,455	$41,993
Tax Savings	-$10,007	-$10,498

Trade-in value after 4 Years	$20,0000	
Equity	$20,000	$0
Total Actual Cost	$32,449	$31,495
Cost Per month	$676	$656
Monthly savings		$20
Total savings		$954
Additional cash flow		$426

In this $50,000 example, the savings per month in cash flow was $426 per month, and after taxes the savings work out to $20 per month or a total of $954 better than financing the vehicle.

Most companies choose to lease to improve their cash flow. As you can see in this example, there was an extra $426 per month of cash flow back into the business. This money can be allocated to purchasing inventory, reducing debt, advertising, or any other way to move the business forward.
If you decide to lease, then the residual value should be at fair market value and not too low, otherwise, the CRA will consider it a finance purchase and not allow you to write it off as a lease. The best way to choose a residual value is to look at what similar 4-5 years old vehicles are worth on the resale market today, (Trader.ca or Canadian Black Book), and see if it is in line with what the leasing company is proposing. It is best to have a lower residual at the end of your lease giving you some equity than it is to have a high residual and run the risk of having to

pay money to return the vehicle at the end of the lease.

Commercial lines of credit

Commercial lines of credit are great for growing businesses and they can be set up ahead of time prior to purchasing your vehicles. Most lines of credit usually start from $250,000 and can go up to a million dollars and give the company the flexibility to purchase vehicles as they are needed without the constant paperwork of a single purchase. These lines of credit are perfect for companies that buy five or more vehicles per year. Many of my clients are now going this route. I will negotiate rates on their behalf along with the terms, and they can then purchase any vehicle or equipment and do not have to go through the approval process every time.

You can even choose which type of purchasing - financing or leasing - you would like available on the lines of credit. Consider this as money when you need it which does not tie up your operating lines of credit.

5. How to Get the Best Price, Guaranteed!

The best thing you can do for yourself is to secure financing *prior* to looking for a vehicle. This way you have the funds in place, and when you make a decision you'll have negotiation power.

There are commercial lenders that will pre-approve you for a finance, lease, or even establish a line of credit prior to purchasing a vehicle. These lines of credit can be used for vehicles or equipment and give you flexibility in the case of an emergency.

Getting approved for a commercial loan is not always easy and should not be left to the last minute.

What you will need to apply for a loan:

- Credit application.
- Articles of incorporation.
- Void check.
- Two years of financials (audited statements are best).
- Guarantors for the loan. (may be required)
- Previous vehicle loan information.
- Trade references.

If you can walk in already approved, you can call the shots. If you don't like the rate offered by the dealer, you can ask for a better one. If you don't like the terms, you can change them.

The secret is that if your loan is handled correctly and you are prepared, the banks will compete with one another to lend you money. Knowing the best lenders and shopping the market for your needs can make all the difference.

Get the lowest price on any vehicle

If the price is the most important thing to you, and you want to save the most money and get a great deal on a new vehicle, it's going to take a little bit of work.

You must do the research in your marketplace.

First, get the price of the vehicles that you're interested in, as well as the discounts including the rebates (individual and fleet) and the interest rates. You must also find out which rebates are compatible with one another. Sometimes you can combine interest rates and rebates, and sometimes you cannot.

You can get some of this information by visiting websites and making phone calls but to get all the financial data, you will most likely have to visit several dealerships and talk to a number of salespeople. Not all salespeople and managers know their own programs, so you may have to compare information from several dealerships.

Once you have all the financial information, you will need to compile it in a spreadsheet to compare the data. By comparing pricing, options, and interest rates along with the resale data, you can approximate the true cost of a vehicle today and what it will be worth the day that you trade or sell it.

You want to look for the vehicle with its price and resale value close to each other. In other words, selling price - trade value = true cost.

Once you have selected a vehicle that you're interested in purchasing, it's time to go visit the dealers again. Get the dealers to give you their best pricing and put it in writing.

You may have to go to four or five dealers, as many of them will not give you their best pricing unless you're willing to buy the vehicle that same day. If you have a trade-in, keep that separate from the new vehicle purchase as that is a different transaction altogether.

Get the dealers to give you prices *without* a trade-in. You want to know how much the new vehicle is without a trade-in. Once you have agreed on the selling price, then you can get bids on your trade-in. That may require you to go back to the top three dealers from whom you got the best prices, and have them appraise your vehicle.

When you're done, you'll have the lowest price on the new vehicle and the highest trade-in value on your old vehicle. Sounds easy, doesn't it?

Get the most for your trade

Getting a trade value on your current vehicle can sometimes be a challenge. You can get a lot of opinions; however, you want somebody who will write a cheque.

There are many websites that offer prices, such as Canadian Black Book; but determining the trade is not an exact science. There are some software programs available to dealers and brokers that help with this process. Such software looks at all the transaction prices, the listed prices, and the auction results, and gives an estimate. This estimate is based upon the last ninety days of transactions and is just a reference point to work from.

Determining the values of vehicles based on data from websites like autotrader.ca can be even more confusing. The top 25% of vehicles listed are usually overpriced. The bottom 25% usually have something seriously wrong with them. Like with Google reviews, look in the middle, and that's most likely where you will find the true value of your vehicle.

6. Know the Highway Traffic Act and MTO

When operating a commercial vehicle or a fleet of commercial vehicles in the province of Ontario, there are rules you must know and follow.

Gone are the days when you could buy a pickup truck, paint your name on the side of it, and go to work. Thanks to some bad operators, their employees, and people on the public roads who put themselves at risk, there are now a lot of rules for operating a commercial truck.

In Ontario, the Highway Traffic Act (HTA) regulates the licensing of vehicles, classification of traffic offenses, administration of loads, classification of vehicles and other transport related issues.

The Ministry of Transportation of Ontario (MTO) is responsible for transport infrastructure and related law in Ontario.

You need to understand the law and all the meanings of the weights and measures. All measurements are stated in metric system units. In our industry and in this book I sometimes use imperial measurements as a description but the law is in metric.

Weights and measures

Many people get confused by the weight ratings of commercial vehicles and their meanings. Gross vehicle weight (GVW) and gross vehicle weight rating (GVWR) are not exactly the same thing.

The GVW is what the vehicle weighs including its contents.

The GVWR is what the manufacturer has equipped the vehicle to carry, including driver, fuel, truck body, and the payload

The GVWR should not be confused with payload.

Payload is a calculation of the weight of the vehicle, including all of its options and the body, minus the GVWR. For example, let's say you have an 8,845-kilogram GVWR truck (19,500 lbs.). Meanwhile, the empty weight of that vehicle, including the driver, the truck body, and fuel, is 4,309 kilograms (9,500 pounds) GVW. The payload calculation would be 8,845 GVWR – 4,309 GVW = 4,536 kilograms (10,000 pounds) of payload capacity.

All drivers should know the capacity of their trucks on a daily basis. A best practice would be to put all the aftermarket equipment on the truck, fill it with fuel, and weigh the truck. This new curb weight amount should be updated on the ownership. Then take this new weight and deduct the amount from the GVWR from the sticker weight on the door. This will give you the estimated payload of your truck when it is properly loaded.

Place a sticker (use a label maker) on the dash showing the amount that each truck is capable of carrying. This will eliminate unnecessary tickets and allow the driver to know the position of the load and its effect on the weights of each axle. Make sure that all of your drivers understand that the weight needs to be distributed to each axle without exceeding the weight rating on individual axles.

Overloading a vehicle is not only against the law, it is also very dangerous. An overloaded vehicle loses its ability to steer and stop. If overloaded on a regular basis, your vehicle will experience excess wear, lose its longevity, and put at risk your employees and your business.

How about towing? The gross coupled weight rating (GCWR) is provided by the manufacturer, and determines the allowed weight of a truck and trailer combination for that vehicle. This rating is not posted on the vehicle; it will be in the specifications of the newly purchased vehicle. This rating is determined by the size of brakes, payload of the vehicle, axle ratios, and the transmission type.

Class G license: How to stay within the legal weight

In Ontario (other provinces use other classification designations), the majority of drivers on the road have only Class G licenses. A Class G license allows someone to drive a vehicle with a gross vehicle weight (GVW) or a gross coupled weight rating (GCWR) of up to 11,000 kilograms (24,250 pounds). The GVW is the weight of the vehicle and its contents.

For example, for a truck that weighs 4,536 kilograms and is carrying 6,464 kilograms of payload, the GVW is 11,000 kilograms. While the

GVWR could be 11,793 kilograms, as long as the vehicle is licensed for 11,000 kilograms, then that vehicle is legal with a G-license driver.

I get asked all the time if it is possible to carry 5,400 kilograms of payload while pulling a 4,500-kilogram trailer on a Class G license. The answer is no! The limitation of the G license means that any truck that you choose and any option that you add to it affects the payload.

Since there is a limit of 11,000 kilograms, a smaller and lighter truck and a higher GVWR will mean more payload. For a landscaper or light construction worker, typically I recommend either a Class 5 truck with a GVWR of 8,864 kilograms or a Class 6 truck license down to 11,000 kilograms.

If the materials used for the body or flat deck are lighter, this will mean additional payload. A lighter body will also save fuel because the truck is not carrying around the weight of that body when not being used for payload.

Trailers with a Class G license

When considering adding a trailer to a commercial truck, consider that some of the weight of the trailer gets transferred to the truck. Depending on how the trailer is set up, the additional weight will be between ten to twenty percent transferred to the GVW of the towing vehicle. So if the 4,500-kilogram trailer has fifteen percent of its weight going onto the truck, then you have to deduct 675 kilograms from the towing vehicle's maximum payload.

For a G-license driver, the gross combined weight is a factor. You cannot exceed the truck and trailer combination of 11,000 kilograms). The effective weight of the trailer itself and its contents cannot weigh more than 4,600 kilograms. Ten to twenty percent of the weight of the trailer will be transferred to the towing vehicle.

Annual inspection of vehicles (Yellow Sticker)

Trucks and trailers that have a registered gross vehicle weight or a gross vehicle weight of over 4,500 kg require an annual inspection. This includes the combination of the truck and the trailer including the payload in both vehicles

There are three conditions under which a vehicle and trailer will require an annual inspection:

1. The actual weight of the vehicle or the registered gross vehicle weight is over 4,500 kilograms.
2. The gross vehicle weight plus the gross weight of the trailer is over 4,500 kilograms.
3. The gross vehicle weight rating of the truck and the gross vehicle weight rating of the trailer combined exceed 4,500 kg.

The components that will be inspected are:

- Powertrain
- Suspension
- Brakes

- Steering
- Instruments and auxiliary equipment
- Lights
- Electrical systems
- Body
- Tires and rims
- Hitches and couplers

As of January 1, 2016, the scope of the commercial annual inspection has increased and is now more in-depth. Some of these changes include amendments to the suspension component, braking system, steering, body, tire and rim and coupling device inspections and tolerances.

Many of these changes are just common sense and most operators will benefit in the long run as the vehicles will be inspected better and held to a higher standard for road safety.

If either the vehicle or the trailer already has or requires the annual inspection certificate, then both of them must have an annual inspection.

Speed limiters

In Ontario and Quebec, all vehicles with an electronic control module built after December 31st, 1994 having a GVWR over 11,794 kilograms must have a speed limiter. This limiter must restrict the speed of the vehicle to 105 km/h. The exemptions are limited and include ambulances and fire trucks. The fines for non-compliance start at $250 plus court costs. Depending on the scope of the offence the MTO is authorized to charge fines up to

$20,000. This kind of fine would be for multiple offences and would be rare. However, I have heard of an MTO officer in the past laying a $10,000 charge to a carrier for multiple offences and the charges did stick. Needless to say, it is a good idea to obey the law and add the limiter to your older trucks over 11,794 kilograms. Don't tempt fate and you will also save fuel and a bunch of tickets.

Do I need a CVOR?

There is a lot of confusion over the Commercial Vehicle Operator's Registration (CVOR) but I will try to make it as simple as possible. Any operator (company) using a vehicle for commercial purposes with a vehicle gross weight (GVW) or a registered gross vehicle weight (GVWR) over 4,500 kg (9,920.8 lbs.), or any bus with ten or more passengers, must have a CVOR. This includes trucks and trailers.

The CVOR costs $250 to apply for, and you will pay $50 per every year after that. You need to apply through the Ministry of Transportation at www.mto.gov.on.ca. This form must be filled out correctly and completely.

Once you receive your CVOR make sure to keep the following documents in your company vehicles at all time.

- Copy of the CVOR document
- Copy of valid vehicle ownership with signature
- Original insurance pink slip
- Pre-trip daily inspection sheet

- PMCVI annual inspection certificate document
- Daily travel log (if traveling over 160 kilometers from home base or over 15 hours of service)
- Lease agreement (if applicable). Many clients I know have a folder with sheet protectors in the vehicle with all of the documents. It keeps everything in one place and avoids paperwork being lost.

In order to renew your vehicle license plate stickers for commercial vehicles, your CVOR must be kept up-to-date.

Class D license

In Ontario, having a Class D license allows the driver to operate any truck or trailer with a GVW or GCW over 11,000 kilograms (24,250 pounds), provided the trailer and its contents are under 4,600 kilograms (10,141 pounds).

Z-Endorsement

This is required to operate any vehicle with an air braking system (ABS) regardless of any other criteria. Having an air brake license or a Z-endorsement can be independent of the other licensing. For example, you could have a Class G license and a Z-endorsement, which would mean you have a GZ license. The same goes for the other designations.

Class A license

The Class A license is required to operate a vehicle pulling a trailer and contents greater than 4,600 kilograms (10,141 pounds), provided it does not exceed the weight restriction of the manufacturer or the length and width restrictions of the MTO.

Restricted Class A license

The restricted Class A license is a designation for drivers that will be towing smaller trailers with electric brakes that exceed 4,600 kilograms. With a restricted Class A license, the only condition would be that a driver must not operate a motor vehicle pulling double trailers or a trailer with air brakes.

Weigh scales

All commercial vehicles with a CVOR, regardless of size, are required to stop at weigh scales when the amber lights are flashing. This includes pick-up trucks. Basically anything with a yellow sticker on the windshield is required to pull over at the weigh scales. (The only exception is a non-commercial application like renting a cube van to do a personal move.)

Vehicles with snow plows and trailers

Roof clearance lights and rear marker lights must be on every vehicle over 2.06 meters (81") wide. Any truck that has dual rear wheels must have clearance lights, but a pickup truck with a single rear wheel may not. So the list below may apply if you're operating a truck that will be towing a wide trailer.

Most common offences and their fines:

Overloading 0 to 2,499 kg = $4.00 per 100 kg (no less than $100.00).
Overloading from 2,500 kg to 4.999 kg = $5.00 per 100 kg.
Overloading from 5,000 kg to 7,499 Kg = $6.00 per 100 kg.
Insecure load commercial vehicle = $310.00 (N.S.F).
Insecure load for small aggregates (no roll tarp) = $310.00.
No clearance lights on a vehicle over 2.032 m wide (plow truck) = $200.00.

Protecting your CVOR

If your business requires commercial vehicles, then you need to protect your CVOR. This requires understanding the rules and some training. After too many offenses, the ministry will sanction your CVOR and this could inhibit the operation your business. Take a little time to understand the rules, because proper training will make all the difference.

7. The Future of Transportation

When I first started in the car business, having a cassette player with auto reverse in your car was a cool option to have. Now features like self-parking, GPS, and Wi-Fi to stream Netflix to keep the kids happy are ubiquitous. The cost of technology is dropping very quickly, and some of the formerly expensive technologies for fleets have now become more mainstream and almost essential. GPS technology was something that only big corporations could afford for logistics, but now even small landscape companies have GPS just to confirm to their clients the time of arrival at the parking lot for snow removal and the time they started work.

Big Brother

In order to operate a fleet in these days, you'll soon find that you will have front facing cameras and GPS technology in all of your vehicles. This will be to keep track of them and avoid potential lawsuits. The front facing cameras will record video to eliminate any disputes over fault in a collision and the GPS to improve overall logistics for the company.

This is not so you can play Big Brother and spy on employees; rather, it's all about efficiency and lowering costs. It does not make sense to send a technician from twenty kilometers away to do a service call when a technician who is on the next block can solve the problem in five minutes. The only reason a business owner won't do that now is because he (or she) doesn't know the locations of the technicians. With GPS on all the trucks, you can see all of the vehicles' locations and adapt quickly to any given situation.

There are many side benefits to having this technology, such as the ability to quickly pick up parts because one of your trucks is traveling right by the depot, or doing quick deliveries because a truck is making a trip near your client's office.

Once this technology is implemented, fuel costs go down and productivity goes up. Seeing the data can help eliminate aggressive driving habits such as speeding, harsh braking, or excessive idling. There are other benefits, like prevention of fuel and vehicle theft. You can put a virtual barrier/fence along the perimeter of your site, and if your vehicle crosses outside the perimeter without proper authorization, the system will send you an alert. You should know what happens to your vehicles and who is driving them.

Some of these GPS solutions also include preventative maintenance software. A preventative maintenance software system will keep you in control of the maintenance for your vehicles. You can track current costs and predict future costs. This software can alert you based on mileage of future services and warranty expiration dates.

How far away are self-driving vehicles?

In the near future (probably within twenty years from now) we'll be riding around in fully autonomous vehicles. This will be a huge game changer for everyone. Some people think that these cars will be dangerous and they'll start crashing into people.

A century ago, people had similar fears about entering an elevator without an elevator operator. They would take the stairs because they did not trust that the machine could do as good a job as a person. That was a long time ago but it was a real fear for some people.

Self-driving cars will be amazing for many people. Think about the elderly who want their independence but can no longer drive safely. They may be the first adopters of this technology because it will restore their freedom. Taxicabs and limousines will become fully autonomous, picking us up and dropping us off with a touch of an app.

Imagine your trucks picking up your products and delivering them right to your client's warehouse. The trucks show up on time and deliver the loads on time without any incident, working twenty-four hours a day. That scenario might be several years away, but it will certainly be an interesting development.

I think this will affect the car business and change it because cars will become more useful in different ways than our current experiences. We can now drop our kids off at school without actually driving them, we can have the car waiting for us outside our office when we are done for the day instead of walking to the parking lot, we can send the car to go and get the takeout food from the local restaurant have the chef place the food in the trunk and the car can bring our dinner back to us. The possibilities are endless.

I do think that our current relationship with the automobile will change significantly. Owning a car may not be a status symbol anymore or maybe the opposite will be true that having exclusive use of your own car even more desirable.

Car ownership will definitely change, insurance costs should go down, and injuries due to car crashes hopefully will be all but eliminated. I think the technology is exciting and I look forward to it, even though I am a driver at heart.

It's hard to say what the future holds but we do live in interesting times.

8. Working with a Professional

What if there were a better way to buy vehicles for your fleet?

What if business owners could hire somebody to take care of the vehicle purchasing process for them - an industry expert who knew the business inside and out? Someone who would look after the owner's best interests, not just their own? Someone who was on the owner's side in the negotiations?

Companies hire professional brokers for services like insurance, transportation freight, food distribution, and mortgages. These companies hire people with experience because they are experts and they have their fingers on the pulse of their industry, knowing all the market prices and the acceptable rates are for any product. They save you money instead of costing money.

Why not hire a fleet broker?

Would hiring a fleet broker work for you, or would you rather do it yourself?

Lots of vehicle information can be found on the internet for comparing features, horsepower, weights, measurements, pricing, and reliability ratings.

If you put in the time, you can discover it on your own. Typically, to get a fair deal count on at least fifteen to twenty hours, maybe more to do all the research, send emails, make phone calls, and visit dealerships.

If you don't have a lot of time and you also have a fleet of ten or more vehicles, this process can be a lot of work, especially if you go through the steps a few times per year.

The challenge with doing it yourself is the value of your time. If you bill yourself out at $100-$150 per hour, you're losing time and money, and time is the one thing you cannot get back, even if you're a master negotiator who manages to strike an awesome deal every time.

Any of your savings will be lost in your own labor per hour costs. This is why many companies hire specialists to get the same or better results. They will spend less time on vehicle purchasing and more time running their business.

Have someone on your side

In any transaction, there are two interested parties. In this situation, you need a new car or truck for your business, while the dealership has inventory that it needs to sell. The broker is your agent, who works for you and not the dealership. The broker's only interest is getting you the best price and lowering your costs. They negotiate on your behalf for the new vehicle, the trade value, and the financing or leasing rates.

Since all three of these are kept separate, you can realize savings on each part. The price of the new vehicle will be lower, you will see a higher trade-in value through multiple offers, and you will get the lowest interest rate available by shopping the finance market.

Help you stay focused on your business

The most important thing in running a business is to maintain focus on your business and not to get sidetracked. Buying vehicles for your business should be no more emotional than buying a new printer for the office. No one gets emotionally involved in negotiating for a business tool like a printer, but sometimes people get too passionate during the purchase of vehicles.

Being emotional in any business transaction is a loser's game; if you get too wrapped up in winning, then you lose sight of your original goal. Even lawyers, who by virtue of their occupation are master negotiators, know better than to negotiate for themselves. When important personal interests are at stake, they'll hire another lawyer to negotiate for them.

You don't know what you don't know

No one knows what they don't know. I can tell you I know how to change a light bulb and re-wire a lamp, but this doesn't make me an electrician. Even if you have purchased dozens of cars, that doesn't mean you are an industry expert on the automotive market; it just makes you a person involved in numerous automobile transactions.

Malcolm Gladwell told us that in order to truly become an expert on any subject, one must spend at least 10,000 hours on it. Some companies will have the purchasing department do the buying. That makes a lot of sense since they buy things for the company every single day. However, the person who buys laser printer paper and cleaning supplies for the warehouse may not have the skills or knowledge required to make a purchasing decision on a $150,000 commercial vehicle. Why would you ever leave this task to them?

It would only make sense to get the guidance of an industry expert who knows the pricing and the rebates, ways to get all the best deals, and will save you from making all sorts of mistakes.

In addition, being an industry insider, your agent will have additional buying power. You may buy one truck of a particular brand every 2-3 years, while a broker may buy fifty of those trucks within just one year.

Who do you think will get better pricing?

Hidden fleet rebates

Many dealerships are not focused on fleet clients and don't understand the needs of a commercial buyer. Sometimes there are extra rebates offered by the manufacturer that even the selling dealer doesn't know about.

If the dealer selling the vehicle doesn't know about these offers, you certainly will never find out about them.

Knowing the competition

It shocks me that most dealers don't investigate the price at which their competitors sell vehicles. It seems so myopic that they focus only on their own vehicles and interest rates, never looking into the market to find out if they are truly competitive. A broker does this for you as a part of their service.

9. How My Business Works

I deal directly with business owners that need multiple company vehicles. These owners choose to spend their time on their business rather than shopping and negotiating.

Because of my wide range of experience and knowledge of the industry, my product offering runs the entire gamut from cars to heavy trucks.

Should you and I decide to work together, my promise to you will be that I will look after your fleet as if it were my own.

When you decide to become my valued client, here are a few of the dreary tasks I'll take off your back.

No more tedious back-and-forth negotiations

If you bought a vehicle at least once before you must have experienced the back-and-forth negotiations with the sales person who can't make any decision without their manager. You typically only get to meet this manager when they come in at the very end of the negotiation looking for "one last bump". This is an attempt to raise the price at the very last moment of negotiation to sweeten their side of the deal. If you like I can make sure you never get dragged into this most frustrating game ever again.

No more annoying phone calls from salespeople

I'll take away the fifteen to twenty calls per week from various salespeople that call around dinner hour just to see if you "have made up your mind yet"”

No more phony low-ball offers

Most dealers will offer below-market value pricing on your trade in order to initiate negotiation. Unless you start to negotiate with them, often you won’t get the real price for the trade. Combining the selling price, the trade value, and the payments into one number makes it harder for you to figure out the value of any of those components. I will spare you this "shell game" and any of the low-ball offers on your trade-in.

No more wondering if you got a good deal

You won’t lie awake at night wondering if you got a good deal. You’ll sleep soundly *knowing* you got a good deal and you had someone on your side at every step along the way.

Enlisting my help is a simple process.

Step 1: Free consultation

The first step is the initial consultation, which in most cases is absolutely free of charge. We’ll meet in person, on the phone, or online. I'll find out the needs of your company, the application for the vehicle, and your current situation. If we decide to work together, I will act as your agent. It's like having your own fleet manager without paying any salaries. Together we'll go through your budget and discuss all the available options and some new technologies of which you may not be aware of.

Step 2: Trade-ins

If you have a trade-in vehicle, I'll take information to do market research regarding resale values and transaction prices. We'll take photos and do an appraisal of the vehicle, then send it out for bids. Typically, I get three or more bids on any trade from independent buyers to make sure that my client is getting the highest possible trade-in value.

Step 3: Pricing estimates

I'll provide initial pricing estimates based on your needs and your budget, and then suggest appropriate vehicle options to match the initial budget. Then we'll move to the financial approval to secure the funds needed for the purchase and to get the best rate. If you plan on purchasing several times throughout the year, the company could even get approval on a line of credit used for vehicles and equipment.

Step 4: Negotiating with dealers, body manufacturers, and banks

Next we'll typically go into the market and negotiate with the dealers, the body manufacturers, and possibly the vehicle manufacturers, depending on the size of the order.

Step 5: Project management for factory orders and custom vehicles

Sometimes ordering a custom-made commercial truck from the factory can take a long time. There are many decisions that need to be made quickly along the way to keep the new vehicle order moving forward. I work as your project manager on the order. I take care of all the small decisions and get your input for the large ones. Because I am an expert I know the logistics of building a vehicle and coordinate with the dealers, the body manufacturers, and the aftermarket to make sure that all the equipment, options, and components are installed correctly. These decisions keep the completion of the new vehicle on time and on budget.

Step 6: Delivery right to your door!

Once the new vehicle is ready it is delivered right to your home, office, or job site. I take care of everything including all the paperwork related to licensing. My job is to ensure that you have the vehicle you need on time and on budget.

10. Five Things to Know Before Hiring a Broker

There are five things you need to know before you hire a fleet broker. Your broker needs to

#1 Be OMVIC licensed

Automotive brokers in Ontario must be licensed.

The Ontario Motor Vehicle Council (OMVIC) created a new Motor Vehicle Dealer Act of 2002 that laid out the new rules: brokers must be licensed in the same way as dealers. Brokers are required to follow very strict guidelines set out by the industry and the Consumer Protection Act to make sure that customers are being treated fairly and ethically.

By law, brokers must represent their customers and no one else. Brokers cannot be affiliated with any dealer or any manufacturer and must remain completely unbiased in any transaction.

You can confirm registration of any individual broker by visiting OMVIC.ca.

2 Have experience

People can start many businesses without any experience, but automotive brokering is not one of them. Mistakes involving commercial trucks can cost hundreds of thousands of dollars. If your broker gets you a price that is thousands less than quoted elsewhere but orders the wrong truck with the wrong equipment, it could result in a costly disaster. You may not know until after you have taken delivery. Your broker needs to know what he's doing. Check out their credentials and experience prior to doing business with them.

3 Know your industry

Your broker needs to know what your business and your vehicles do every day. He must be familiar with all the weight measurements and laws in your jurisdiction. He must also understand lifecycle costs for repairs, maintenance, and fuel.

4 Be independent

An independent broker cannot work for any dealer or dealership group. A broker who does work for a dealership or a dealer group is a salesperson, not a broker. A broker cannot be affiliated with any dealer, manufacturer, or leasing company. Only complete independence enables brokers to give their clients truly unbiased advice.

5 Have solid references

Before allowing a person to purchase vehicles for your business, ask for references!

In hiring professionals to act on your behalf in all negotiations, you want to make sure that they are legitimate. I would ask for five references and call at least three of them. If they don't have references, then they most likely do not have clients. Ask for references from people who are in your industry. You may know some of them personally.

Look the broker up on LinkedIn

Another good way of reviewing a broker's credentials is to look them up on LinkedIn. See if they share any of your connections. Call those individuals and ask if they have done business with the potential broker and if they think that the broker is honest and trustworthy.

This may seem a little extreme, but you are hiring this person to take care of a very important part of your business and there is a lot of money involved. I would vet that person in the same way that I would vet a senior manager.

11. Frequently Asked Questions

How does a broker get paid?

The selling dealer usually pays the broker's fee and incorporates it into the purchase price.

Do I pay more for a vehicle by using a broker?

In nearly every case, you will pay less. The broker's fee is covered by the additional discounts that I get for my clients.

Don't dealers dislike dealing with brokers?

No, it is quite the opposite. Dealers like selling through professional automotive brokers because the broker does all of the work. The broker has a client who decides on the dealer's vehicle. The broker brings the request for proposal and the dealer bids on the deal with his best wholesale price. The financing is usually pre-approved and the clients are happier. The dealer gets a deal that is usually outside of his area of representation, so it costs him nothing to sell the vehicle. The additional sale helps the dealer to reach his sales targets. Since the clients are so happy with the process, they give the dealer high customer satisfaction scores, and everyone wins.

Why have I never heard of this type of service before?

There are not a lot of commercial brokers and it's not easy to get an OMVIC broker's license. Before they changed the dealer act there were several hundred brokers in the GTA. Now with the

Consumer Protection Act and OMVIC licensing requirements, a broker needs to go through a rigorous vetting process similar to that of a dealer getting a license.

Why shouldn't I just go to the dealer to buy my cars and trucks?

If you want to spend your time running from dealer to dealer to save a little money, then go for it! The advantage is that a broker works for you, not for the dealer. There is no conflict of interest when it comes to getting you the best rates, highest trade value, and lowest pricing on the new vehicle. On the salesperson side of the equation, there are many reasons why this can't happen.

If I buy from a broker, will my vehicle still get good service?

Yes, it will. The warranty on your vehicle is included with the vehicle and applies anywhere in North America. The fact that a professional negotiated and arranged the purchase of your vehicle has no bearing on the quality of service that you will receive. If you are having difficulty with a particular dealer, I will refer you to another dealer and request that they take care of your vehicle as if it had been purchased at their location.

Are there hidden fees or incentives available to brokers only?

No, but there are some manufacturer incentives that even dealers won't know about. Clients often lose out on money that was available to them just because the dealers are not completely up-to-date with their own programs. This extra money may be sitting there but the salesperson or sales manager never applies for it.

My Invitation to You

As a business owner with a fleet of vehicles, you have a lot on your plate. Purchasing a new car or truck for your business these days can be a real hassle. Remember the article in *The Globe and Mail* that said most people would rather clean a toilet than shop for a new car? And they were talking about buying just one car! What if you're a fleet owner and have to do this several times per year?

Are you tired of this yet? Tired of doing all the price comparisons and vehicle research, then never really knowing if you got a good deal or not? Tired of the surprises - and I don't mean "the good type" of surprises - when it comes to the older vehicles in your fleet. Do you want happier employees? Employees that respect the vehicles because they are newer and better looking?

If so, call or email me and tell me a little bit about your business and what your goals are. I will share with you some ideas on how to improve your current situation. If it looks like I can help you and we decide to work together, I will put together an action plan that will make you more efficient, save you a ton of time, and make you more money. The best part is you get to go back to running your business again.

Client Testimonials

"In the last 25 years I have dealt with a dozens of fleet managers. Many of them it seemed, cared little about the challenges we face in the car rental business.

When I met Sean he was different, he asked a lot of questions and wanted to know more about my business model. Most of all, he wanted to know what was important to me! I told him, I want to have "the ability to predict the future". I was kind of kidding but not really. What I wanted to know was, before I buy a vehicle am I making the right decision? Will I make a profit on the rental & resale of the vehicle? All of these things are really important when you're running a large fleet of luxury vehicles.

What Sean did next was completely unexpected! He developed for us an entire purchasing system, one that we use for every purchase decision today. Now we just key in the fleet cost, the term, our fixed expenses and we get the answer…is it a good purchase or not? We can actually "predict the future". We know based current market conditions if the vehicle will be profitable or not, right down to the cost per day. There is no more guesswork!

Sean has been invaluable to our company and I'm sure glad that I met him!"

James Schwehr
Affinity Luxury Car Rental

"Purchasing vehicles is a huge undertaking financially. I spend hundreds of thousands of dollars annually and managing those purchases with Sean. He has made all the difference in the world. Sean's attention to detail and guiding us to the right vehicles has helped our business grow. I strongly endorse and support Lockhart Consulting!"

Ed Gibbs
The Gib-San Group

"At Oriole we have had the pleasure of doing business with Sean for over 12 years now. He has helped us get the right truck with the right specs. Sean has been honest with us and has prevented us from making short-sighted decisions when purchasing. Yes, we may have paid initially a little more for the recommended added equipment we got way more in return. Best Value in the business... I wouldn't buy my trucks through anyone else. When it came to leasing... Sean was way better than the competition in getting us set up with the right deal. In the end Sean saves us money and a ton of time."

George Urvari
Oriole Landscaping

"Lockhart Consulting provided us with seamless results directing us in the right direction on the refrigeration units. Professional and thorough, he delivered exactly what we needed. Putting full trust in him was a good move."

Jacob Luss
Shefa Meats

"I have been in the car rental business for the last 17 years and I was doing my own vehicle procurement and disposal. The amount of time I was spending just to buy and sell my cars was getting to be too much. I have since decided to change my process and outsource the procurement task to Lockhart Consulting. I have been really happy with the results. Sean's process is simple, all the vehicle purchasing and disposal logistics are taken care of. Now I get to do what I do best, run my business and rent more cars."

Arun Bansal
Canada Car Rental

"When I first met Sean my company had only one half-ton truck. He has been supporting our growing fleet for over ten years consulting on and supplying multiple new OEM acquisitions as well as a few used vehicles when circumstances dictated. We now run close to 10 vehicles and do so with great efficiency. Sean's advice has always been prompt and sound. He has been an invaluable resource as we plan our growth and our fleet expansion."

Jonathan Auger
Juiceworks Exhibits

"2009 was the last time that I ever walked into a dealership and the first time I met Sean who was then the fleet sales manager at the dealership. My purchase (I say 'my purchase' and not 'Sean's sale' because that is how I felt) was handled so professionally that I was completely mesmerized by Sean's integrity, knowledge and service. I have never felt the need to go to a dealership again for any of my vehicle purchases. I have added at least six more vehicles since and will continue to do so by utilizing Sean Lockhart of Lockhart Consulting as my "go-to guy." In my experience, Sean's services not only save me time and money but also help me make the right choices when it comes to buying and adding vehicles for my business in utility (choosing the right vehicle) and financial aspects."

Gurby Singh Bhatti
GSB Steel Limited

"I have been dealing with Sean since 2003, and I continue to do business with him to this day. Over the years Sean has saved me a lot of time and headaches. He knows exactly what my business needs, and he takes care of everything, from the trade-ins to the leasing, and even custom equipment. His new company is truly outstanding and delivers on its promises. What I like most is, once I explain what it is that I want Sean just takes care of it.

"The only thing I have left to do is just be there in my yard when the new truck arrives. Thanks, Sean, your word is your bond and you stand behind what you say."

Sal Fratangeli
Silverbel Landscaping

"Great to work with you Sean! You are friendly, responsive and professional. Best of all the truck came exactly when you said it would!"

Eleanor Duthie
Stonehenge Design and Build

"The best way to buy a vehicle is to just call Sean. He does everything else. The vehicle just arrives at your door exactly as it was ordered. In the past 15 years, we have purchased many commercial and personal vehicles through Sean including a highly customized F-150 pickup truck. We would have never owned a truck like this without his guidance and expertise. I tell everyone to call Sean."

Garry Hansford
Triple H Paving Stone

Thank You for Reading This Book

Thank you for taking the time to read this book. I hope that you have enjoyed it and learned something new in the process. It has been said that if you want to learn about any subject, the best way to go about it is to teach it. This could not be more true for me writing this book. I have been in the auto business for a little over 25 years, and I thought I knew a lot. It turns out there were many things I didn't know or was clearly misinformed about.

The process of writing a book and doing all the research was a great experience for me. I learned way more than I expected to in this process. I believe that knowledge is power and should be shared with everyone who needs it. I am glad that you picked up this book and had the opportunity to read it.

When I work with companies with their fleets I get an opportunity to make an impact on not just the company but also the people that work there. I get to help my clients and their employees make more money, keep their business running better, and make their lives and jobs easier. I really love what I do!

Thank you,
Sean Lockhart

Save Time, Lower Costs and Improve Productivity

Business owners who have a fleet of vehicles need new tools and strategies to remain competitive in the current business environment. With added competition and shrinking margins, you need a clear and reliable path to follow. Stop the crisis management and make clearer decisions that will grow your business and get the most out of your vehicles.

This book will show you how to:

- Maintain and update your fleet while reducing your overall costs
- Make the small changes that have the biggest payoffs
- Follow the rules of the road for commercial vehicles and fleets in Ontario
- Find an automotive professional that will save you time and get you back to running your business
- Use proven strategies and the latest technology to add to your bottom line

Now you can manage your fleet like the pros, make more money and watch your team become more productive in the process.

To learn more and better manage your fleet, please contact Sean Lockhart at 1-800-476-8407 or email at **info@thefleetbook.com**

62577265R00041

Made in the USA
Charleston, SC
19 October 2016